HISTORY

OF THE

LONDON WATER SUPPLY,

FROM THE

CREATION OF MAN

TO

A.D. 1884.

BY

ADAM GLADSTONE.

PRICE SIXPENCE.

LONDON.

1884.

HISTORY

OF THE

LONDON WATER SUPPLY,

FROM THE

CREATION OF MAN TO A.D. 1884.

THE geographical position of London and the geological formation of its soil demonstrate conclusively that long anterior to the date of the creation of man there was a good water supply in London.

How early in the history of the human race the descendants of our first parents came to London is not known. The authentic history of this great Metropolis is comparatively modern, and I must not indulge that secret and perhaps unconscious desire of flattering the propensity in human nature to venerate antiquity, which has prompted many not only to preserve what is good rather than fly to what is new and untried, but to indulge in the most absurd inventions for the sake of assigning a very early period to the establishment of London as a centre of British polity, industry, and local self-government. Thus Geoffrey of Monmouth, as he is called, a monk who wrote in the twelfth century, ascribes, on the authority of an ancient British manuscript by Walter, Archdeacon of Rhydycen (Oxford), and written about the fourth century, the foundation of the City of London to Brute, a descendant of Æneas, who migrated to this country, according to his relation, about half a century after the destruction of Troy; and he reckons from him seventy kings who reigned successively before the arrival of Julius Cæsar.

There are men who deny to London so ancient a history, and ignore altogether traditions of a date anterior to the invention of letters; but there are many others great and good, including Lord Coke and Bishop Gibson, the editor of *Camden's Britannia*, who favour these ancient legends.

It is sufficient for my purpose to point out that neither in the legendary nor the authentic history of our Metropolis does there appear ever to have been a time before the arrival of Julius Cæsar when the inhabitants found a scarcity of water.

It is quite true that when Cæsar came to Britain our British forefathers were not probably large consumers of water, either for domestic or sanitary purposes, but every man had what he required. As there were no houses, there were no cisterns, no fittings and no water rates. Cæsar says a British town was no more than a " thick wood fortified by a ditch and a mound." The ditch served the double purpose which in our times is served by our rivers and streams; for notwithstanding the boasted advancement of the race during twenty centuries, the local sanitary authorities are still the great enemies of those who supply water, because, for economical reasons, they have converted the pure aqueducts which Nature has provided into carriers for filth.

At that early period, Cæsar tells us, our British forefathers were but half-clothed, and that with skins of beasts. They dwelt in huts built of hurdles and mud, which were the only kind of habitation they were capable of rearing.

What an amount of history can be written on a single page, if it is only sufficiently condensed!

From the time when the ancient British water-carrier dipped his pail of reeds into the ditch near his hut to obtain his daily supply of water to this year of grace 1884, there has been one long battle between those whose desire is to secure a wholesome supply of water and those who pollute the natural sources of such supply. If there had been a Royal Commission of Ancient Britons, they would have used similar language regarding the pollution of their ditches as the Royal Commission now sitting has just used regarding the pollution of the Thames and the Metropolitan Board of Works, the great sewage authority of London. The Commission find that "the discharge of sewage in its crude state during the whole year, without any attempt to render it less offensive by separating the solid or otherwise, is at variance with the original intention and with the understanding in Parliament when the Act of 1858 was passed." "The discharge from the main outfalls becomes very widely distributed by the motions of the water, both up and down the river, being traced in dry seasons through the Metropolis, and almost as high as Teddington."

If the crude sewage of a city with a population of more than four millions can, without serious ill-effects, be poured into the Thames, and after oscillating up and down the river for fifteen miles or more, form foul banks of mud, it is plain that the whole theory and practice of modern sanitary improvement must be a mockery, a delusion, and a costly humbug. Yet the Royal Commission now sitting say such are the facts produced under the modern legislation of 1858 by that ne'er-do-well Board, the Metropolitan Board of Works. It is a most serious thing for the ratepayers to find, after a quarter of a century's trial, that this Board has blundered in every important work it has undertaken.

Some say, as the present Postmaster-General did when the Board wanted to tamper with water supply, " The Board is already overworked, and it would be unwise to throw upon it this additional duty." If this be so, why not reduce its duties, so that the public may have something done as it ought to be?

What of the times before the Metropolitan Board, when London had but one Government, and that the grand old Corporation? Of times when the Lord Mayor and Aldermen, riding forth on horseback, with their ladies following in wagons, took their annual survey of the conduits, after which they used to hunt the hare across the neighbouring fields, then dine with the Chamberlain, after dinner go to hunting the fox, and after " great hallooing at his death and blowing of hornes" ride back through London to the Mansion House? This was before the advent of the water-mill at London Bridge, or the water

schemes of the great Master Myddelton. Then there
were no Medical Officers of Health or Sanitary In-
spectors connected with London government. The
slender streams brought into the City by the conduit
hardly furnished the population with water enough
"for the poor to drinke and the rich to dress their
meate." The cost of water carriage rendered thorough
ablution an impossibility to the indigent, and even to
the wealthiest an occasional and expensive indulgence.
As for street-washing it was never thought of, but left
to the casual operation of the rain. The gutters were
black lines of stagnant filth, which every shower bore
downwards to the lower levels, and washed ultimately
into the river. Heaps of refuse, cabbage-leaves and
cinders, lay rotting in every part of the City even
before the dwellings of noblemen and prelates. No
wonder that the strong and bold "took the wall" of
the weak in their walks through the City, shouldering
the more timid pedestrians aside towards the pestifer-
ous kennel, in which, as Dean Swift vividly records,

"Sweepings from butchers' stalls, dung, guts, and blood,
Drowned puppies, stinking sprats, all drenched in mud,
Dead cats and turnip-tops come tumbling down the flood!"

But we must return to the details of our history
of London water supply rather than pursue the
equally interesting history of those governing bodies
through whose guilt of omission and commission this
water supply has been constantly contaminated.

We will leave the Ancient Britons and the period
of the Roman occupation with but one further re-
mark: that the engineering ability of the Romans
was not required in London to provide aqueducts

such as in other parts of Europe are monuments of Roman civilisation, because here there were wells and streams of pure water amply sufficient for all purposes.

Down to the thirteenth century Londoners knew only this primitive mode of supply; and with pail and pitcher they were wont to resort to the shores of the Thames, to Wall-brook, to Old-bourne, to Long-bourne, to Holy-well, Clements-well, Clerken-well, and other places for their supplies.

The second period in the history of London water supply commenced with the artificial conduit system. In 1235, when the encroachment of buildings and the heightening of the ground had spoiled or dried up many of the fountains and rivulets, causing a dearth of water which the rapid growth of population still further increased, we find the Lord Mayor and Commonalty, at the request of King Henry III., engaged in bringing fresh supplies from the town of Tyburn by six-inch pipes of lead, and setting about the erection of a great stone cistern lined with lead and handsomely castellated, for the public use in Westcheap.

This—the " Great Conduit," as it was called—was the first of its kind in London, and its tedious and expensive construction occupied fifty years. As the population increased, and the old sources of supply became more and more contaminated with sewage, more distant springs at Highbury, Paddington, Hackney, and Hampstead were laid under contribution and brought in earthern pipes, brick drains, or tubes of lead to the City.

For more than three centuries the Lord Mayor and Commonalty, aided by the private gift of many worthy citizens, continued to supply London with water; but so wretched was the supply, and so neglected were the conduits and other means of supply, that at the period of the invention of the lift-pump in 1425 London was in the semi-barbarous condition described by Swift and others in this respect. The pump shared the common fate of new inventions, and was slow to win popular acceptance.

In 1580 Peter Morris took a lease from the Lord Mayor and Aldermen of the first arch of London Bridge for five hundred years at ten shillings a year, and there built his famous water-mill for pumping Thames water into the City. Elm-wood mains and lead pipes conveyed the water to the houses of Londoners, and "my Lord Maior and Aldermen" came in state to witness the first water monopolist throw a jet of water over the steeple of the church of St. Magnus. The conception, grand as it was, did not exceed the grievous necessities of the times; for the water supplied by Morris from the Thames, besides being limited in quantity, was often exceedingly turbid and foul, and the unspeakable squalor of the poor occasioned well-grounded apprehensions that the plague—in those days a fearful sojourner in London—would renew its dreadful visitations. Moved by such considerations, the Corporation had already, towards the end of Elizabeth's reign, obtained power from Parliament to cut a river for conveying water to the City from any part of Middlesex or Hertfordshire. This done, they rested on their oars with true corporate procrastination for six or seven years, till suddenly in 1603 the plague broke out, and raged

with such virulence that in one week it carried off
upwards of a thousand persons in the Metropolis.

Thus fearfully admonished for their wretched procrastination, the Government of London were roused,
and sent surveyors to examine the springs and
water sources round London, to see where water
could be obtained, and having, after much delay,
fixed on the springs of Amwell and Chadwell, in
Hertfordshire, as sufficiently copious and pure for
their purpose, they obtained in 1607 a new Act,
authorising the conveyance of these waters by an
aqueduct to the City. Meantime, the horrors of the
plague had gone, and two years of that vacillation
and debate so characteristic of such bodies followed.

Notwithstanding the corporate wealth, their cour-
age failed, and they made over to Master Myddelton
the power to construct the New River, with any profit that might accrue from the enterprise. There
were vested interests then. Toll were taken—perhaps, by Common Councillors—for the use of convenient dipping-places in the Thames and the streams
flowing into it.

Peter Morris and Bevis Bulmar and others joined
with the common Londoners in jeering at the madcap
scheme of Myddelton. He was harassed with vexa-
tious obstructions of the owners of land across which
he had to cut his trench. After the civil impediments
came the physical difficulties of the enterprise, and
foremost among them the undulations of the ground,
which obliged the projector, for the even distribution
of the flow, to give his channel so devious and me-
andering a course, nearly doubling the crow-flight

estimation of its length and the computed cost of the work, so that by the time Myddelton had brought it to Enfield, just about half-way to London, his progress was stopped by exhaustion of funds. Myddelton pleaded the final success of his scheme before the wise and rich men of the City, but without avail. Scorned by the people themselves, he went to their representatives, the Lord Mayor and Corporation, and before them pleaded the advantages of a good and sufficient water supply, and the duty of the local authority to assist him in securing it, but all to no purpose. The Corporation met the application with a distinct refusal. Myddelton, in his exigency, applied to the canny King, and he, with characteristic rapacity, offered his help, on condition that a moiety of the concern should be made over to him for his exclusive profit and emolument. To these hard terms Myddelton perforce acceded; and subsequently James the King granted their valuable charter to James the Trader and Company, under the title of the New River Company. With the money provided by the King, Myddelton, resuming his operations with his wonted energy, finally completed the work in 1613, twelve months before the expiration of the term allotted for its achievement. It was a great day for the lovers of pomp and show when Royal and civic personages of high dignity assembled at Clerkenwell to see the flood-gates opened and the stream run gallantly into the cistern, amidst the triumphal sounds of drums and trumpets, eighty-five feet above the mid-tide level of the Thames. The New River Company still hint that London should be grateful for all this work of their founder; for in the dingy room where appellants wait before admission to the august Board of Directors, there is a picture of this day of rejoicing, when Myddelton was overwhelmed with laudations as excessive in their warmth as the previous discountenance had been in its coldness. The rash and ruined schemer was now a " magniminous genius," and his achievement was not only · immortal," but even " god-like."

Myddelton was not only a shrewd practical man, with a clear eye for the main chance, but he was a quiet Christian gentleman of high moral character, seldom absent on Sundays from his accustomed seat in St. Matthew's, Friday Street. He knew what a blessing his work would be to plague stricken London, to the poor, whom lovers of wealth and ease had robbed of their natural supplies of water. He mistrusted the notorious selfishness and rapacity of his Royal associate, and, dividing his moiety of the concern into thirty-six shares, he not only proceeded to retrieve his fortune, but, in conjunction with his new partners, he contrived to exclude his Royal associate from any share in the management; and in the Royal charter which incorporated the Company in 1619, there was an express clause reserving to the proprietors of the " Adventurers' Shares," so called in contradistinction to those held by the King and his assigns, all powers of management.

The great Company then formed had the Metropolitan water trade almost entirely to itself for nearly a century. Morris and his family continued the water-wheel at London Bridge, and subsequently the concern was sold to a company, and extended, the Corporation granting three more arches of the bridge on leases similar to the first—which leases the City had to redeem at a heavy cost to the public, when it became necessary to pull down old London Bridge, and to remove the water-wheels beneath it.

The Chelsea Company was the second Water Company, and was established in 1723. This Company just one hundred years ago introduced steam-power into the water service, by substituting one of Boulton and Watt's condensing-engines for the tidal-wheel which had previously worked their pumps.

Since the commencement of the present century three new Companies—the West Middlesex, the East London, and the Grand Junction—have been formed on the north of the Thames, and three—the Vauxhall, the Lambeth, and the Kent—on the south.

In 1810 the principle of competition amongst the Companies suddenly broke out, and was encouraged by the Legislature; but it was soon seen that the public were the losers by such a system, and the Companies ceased this warfare in 1817.

In 1821 the first Parliamentary investigation took place.

During the sixty years that have since elapsed there have been Royal Commissions, Parliamentary inquiries, Water Bills, and schemes, to bring rivers and lakes from distant parts, with reports and pamphlets by thousands, experts on each occasion showing, on the one side, the excellence of the London water supply, and, on the other, the hardships of poor Londoners who are compelled to drink the

" sewer - tainted liquid " supplied by the " Water-mongers' Monopoly."

Amidst reports and suggestions, the Companies have held their own and prospered. It has been very hard at times to withstand the daring statements of opponents, and public opinion has frequently condemned the Companies unheard. The old cries are always re-appearing, perhaps in new forms : Why should London wait ? Why not abolish the water monopoly ? Create a water trust. Empower the Corporation or the Metropolitan Board to buy up the Companies, and give London a wholesome and constant supply, such as is given in many a provincial town.

Manchester manages its own water business ; why should not London do so ?

These are all questions and suggestions which assume that London is badly served.

The magnitude and requirements of London are not considered when talking of Manchester and smaller provincial towns. The special requirements and the special government of London place the Metropolis beyond comparison with the provincial towns, where the water supply is in the hands of the municipal authorities.

There are only five out of the two hundred and seventy Parliamentary and Municipal Boroughs in England and Wales which exceed in population the smallest district supplied by a separate Metropolitan Water Company.

Only two of the Water Companies supply populations less than three hundred thousand persons, and the two largest—the New River and East London—supply a district containing a population equal to that of the five largest towns in England, the New River Company alone supplying a population equal to that of Liverpool and Manchester united.

The area supplied by the eight Water Companies is about forty times that of Liverpool and Manchester, and extends far beyond the area of the Metropolitan Board of Works.

As to the quality of the water between 1828 and the present time, numerous official reports have been made by Royal Commissions, Select Committees, and other public authorities, all tending to show that the present sources of supply are, if the water be properly filtered, as good as any others, and far more convenient. The Duke of Richmond's Commission in 1866 said, "That the abundance, permanence, and regularity of supply, so important to a large metropolis, are secured much more efficiently by the great extent and varied geological character of a large hydrographical basin, such as the Thames, than by the necessarily very much more limited collecting areas that can be made available on the gravitation system." . . . "Further, that there is no evidence to lead us to believe that the water now supplied by the Companies is not generally good and wholesome."

Mr. Ayrton's Committee said in 1867: "We are satisfied that both the quantity and quality of the water supplied from the Thames are so far satisfactory that there is no ground for disturbing the arrangements made under the Act of 1852, and that any attempt to do so would only end in entailing a waste of capital and an unnecessary charge upon the owners and occupiers of property in the Metropolis."

As Dr. Frankland and all other official water

examiners agree, the water is better now than then; *à fortiori* such a committee would be satisfied now.

· Continuous efforts have been made, under the provisions of the Thames Conservancy Acts, to improve the condition of the Thames; and if, as may be hoped, an enlightened Municipality should ere long take the place of the present sewer authorities, and London sewage be dealt with otherwise than for the purpose of polluting the Thames, still greater improvement in the water may be expected.

Since 1852 the Metropolitan Water Companies have not been allowed to take water from the Thames below Teddington Lock, or from any part of the tributary streams within the range of the tide. The wisdom of this is demonstrated by the recent report of the Royal Commission on Sewage Discharge. The improvement in the sanitary laws and the increasing powers of sanitary authorities, and especially the action of the Conservators of the Thames, have had a great effect in preventing the passing of sewage, or other offensive or injurious matter, into the river above the intake of the Water Companies.

The Companies have spent, and are spending, large sums of money in preventing the pollution of the natural sources of water. If Parliament would prevent the Metropolitan Board of Works and the other local sanitary bodies along the Thames, the Lea, and other sources of water, from discharging sewage into the rivers, the Water Companies could provide water at less cost for filtration.

Notwithstanding all their difficulties, the Companies are, according to the official returns (see Dr. Frankland's report to the Local Governmen

Board, 8th February 1884) supplying 140,000,000 gallons a day, or more than thirty gallons a day per head, of a quality and at a price per gallon which compares favourably with any other supply in the kingdom. In Liverpool, Manchester, Glasgow, and other places it is often urged that the water-rates are less than in London, whilst there is a constant supply in those towns. This is true; but it is also true that the habits and requirements of Londoners are such that the consumption of water per head is nearly twice as much in London as in those towns.

It is difficult to see how the sources of London water supply could be improved by theorists. The water from brooks and rivers is condemned by one because, "from the very nature of the case, simple surface supplies are always impure. The surface wash of every section of the country is largely contaminated with vegetable and other organic matter, and is seldom in any sense fit for domestic use." Another condemns the supply from deep wells and borings, because "of the large amount of mineral matter they usually carry." The water of shallow wells is also condemned, because "it is found that the upper levels of all subterranean water strata are contaminated by the drainage of all the filth of the vicinity."

It must be concluded that water, to be fit for domestic uses, must be considered as a manufactured article, and that as much depends upon the processes of filtration and other means of purification as upon the sources of supply.

A year or two ago the amount invested by shareholders in the London Companies was valued at more than thirty millions of money. Even this sum decreases in magnitude when considered with the work done; and this is the only way to understand such large figures.

The annual value of property in the Metropolitan water area, according to the valuation lists, exceeds thirty millions; so that a single rate of twenty shillings in the pound would provide a fund for the purchase of all the interests of the Companies.

For a year's rent a 30*l.* householder would buy his share of the total value of the Companies. It is to be hoped, however, that when such a proposal is again made, it will be made by a truly Municipal body having the confidence of the people. Ratepayers know by sad experience how many millions have been spent in London during the last few years by local bodies, and with such unsatisfactory returns.

The persons who are ready to give their time to the public without some substantial return "in meal or malt" are very few, so that London government, as it is, is largely in the hands of jobbers with talent and their followers without. Good government is worth paying for; and whether the government of the water supply of London is paid for through directors and shareholders, it is a gain to the public so long as we have value for money.

Few men would agree to put the London and North-Western Railway under the management of the Lord Mayor and Aldermen or of the best Vestry or Board of Guardians in England, or even under the Metropolitan Board of Works, who are the picked men of London vestrydom. No, in railway matters, as in water business, we had better bear the ills we have than fly to others we know not of.

Milton Keynes UK
Ingram Content Group UK Ltd.
UKHW020835131124
2812UKWH00039B/161